WHO'S WHO IN THE ZOO

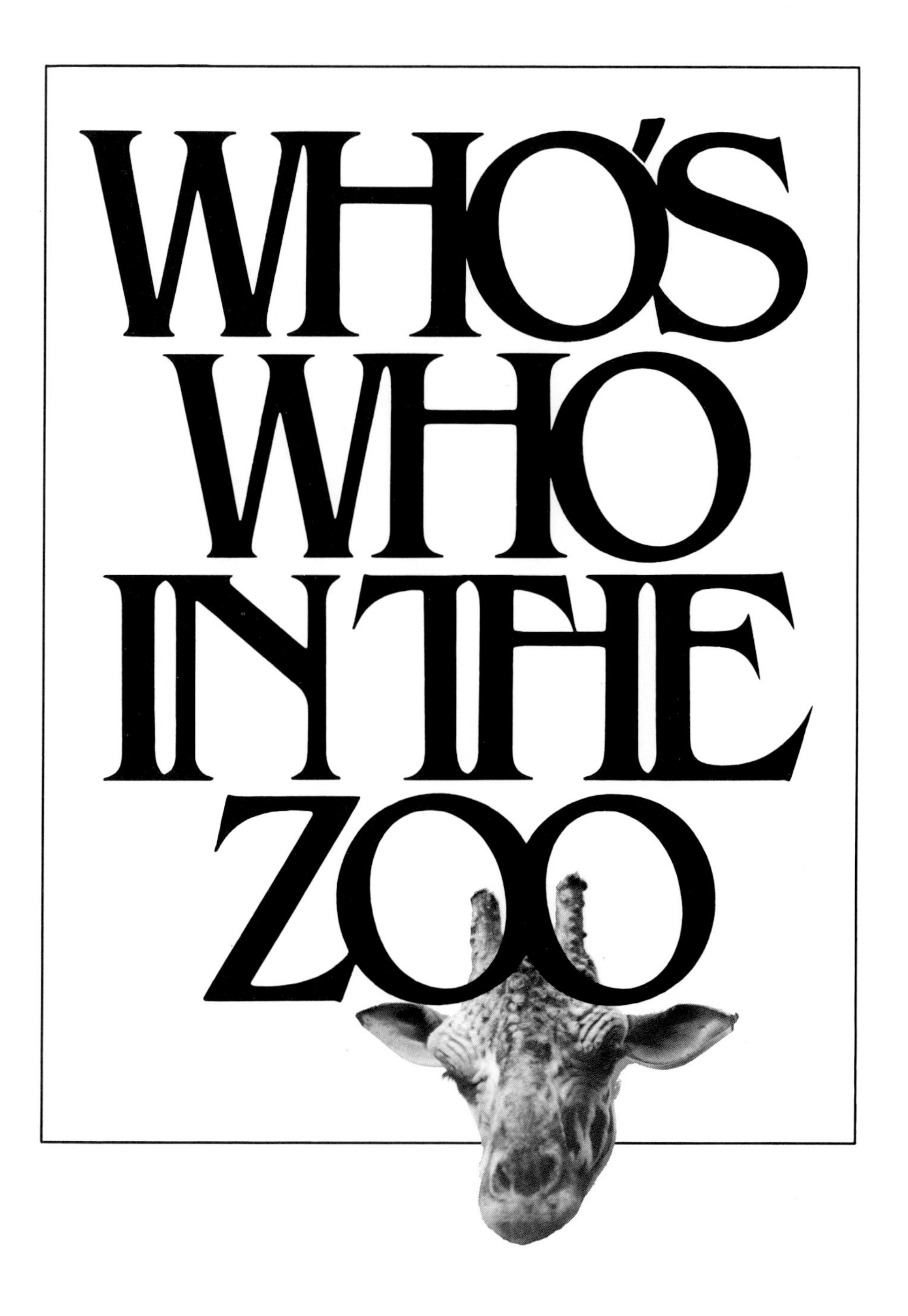

BY LINELL SMITH
PHOTOGRAPHS BY SALLY FOSTER

Oak Tree Publications, Inc.
San Diego, California

First Edition
Manufactured in the United States of America

For information write to:
Oak Tree Publications, Inc.
P.O. Box 1012
La Jolla, California 92038

Library of Congress Cataloging in Publication Data

Smith, Linell Nash.
Who's who in the zoo.

Summary: An introduction to the animals of the zoo using partial pictures and rhyming descriptions to entice the reader to turn the page for a full-page photo of the animal.
1. Zoo animals — Juvenile literature. [1. Zoo animals] I. Foster, Sally, 1937- II. Title.
QL77.5.S58 599 81-1836
ISBN 0-916392-78-3 AACR2

1 2 3 4 5 6 7 8 9 84 83 82 81

Our thanks to the Baltimore Zoo and
the National Zoo for their cooperation.

WHO'S WHO IN THE ZOO

My walk's a miracle of grace.
Soft paw, sharp claw—
A kingly mane surrounds my face.
I roar as back and forth I pace.
Who am I?

Lion

I come from "down under" and jumping's my game.
My takeoff is just like a rocket.
A question that might help you guess my right name
Is, "What have I got in my pocket?"
Who am I?

Kangaroo

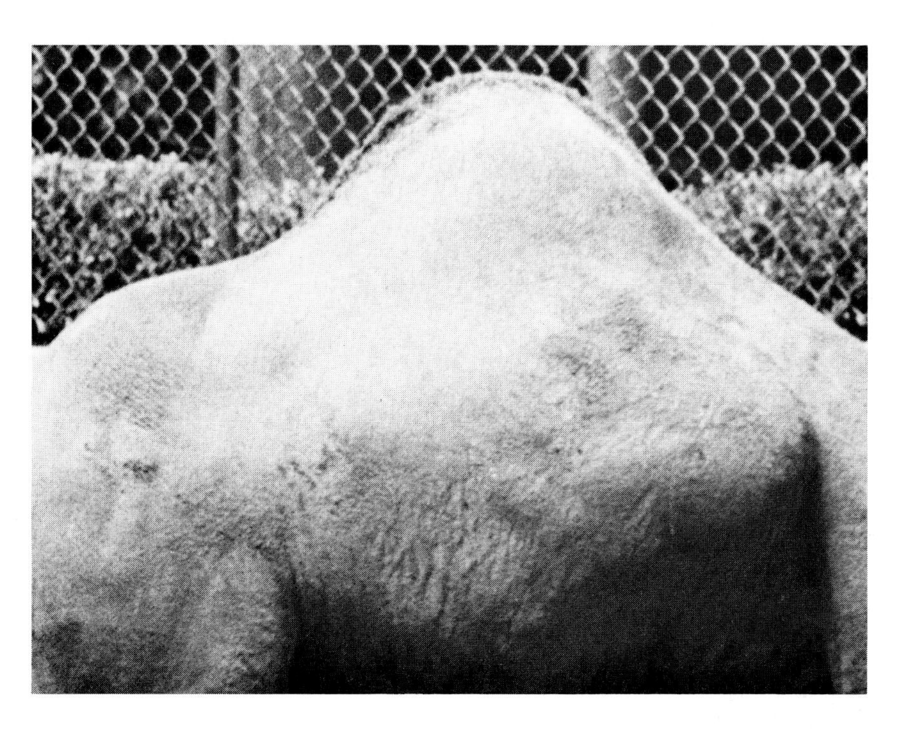

I'm sometimes called a desert ship,
In sand I never sink.
I've got a lumpy humpy back
And seldom need a drink.
Who am I?

Camel

Up, up through the branches I swing to the sky;
My tail is an extra hand.
Then down I come chattering, laughing at life,
With more of my noisy band.
Who am I?

Monkey

I carry luggage everywhere,
My skin's too big for me.
And you will find a mastodon
Upon my family tree.
Who am I?

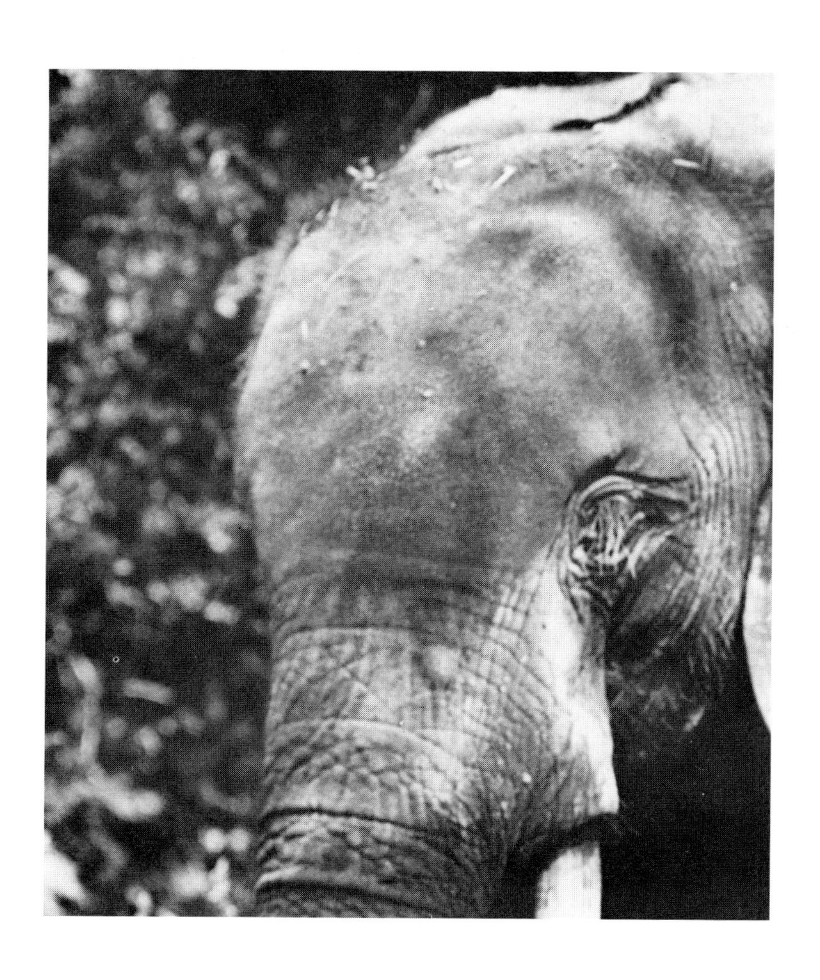

Elephant

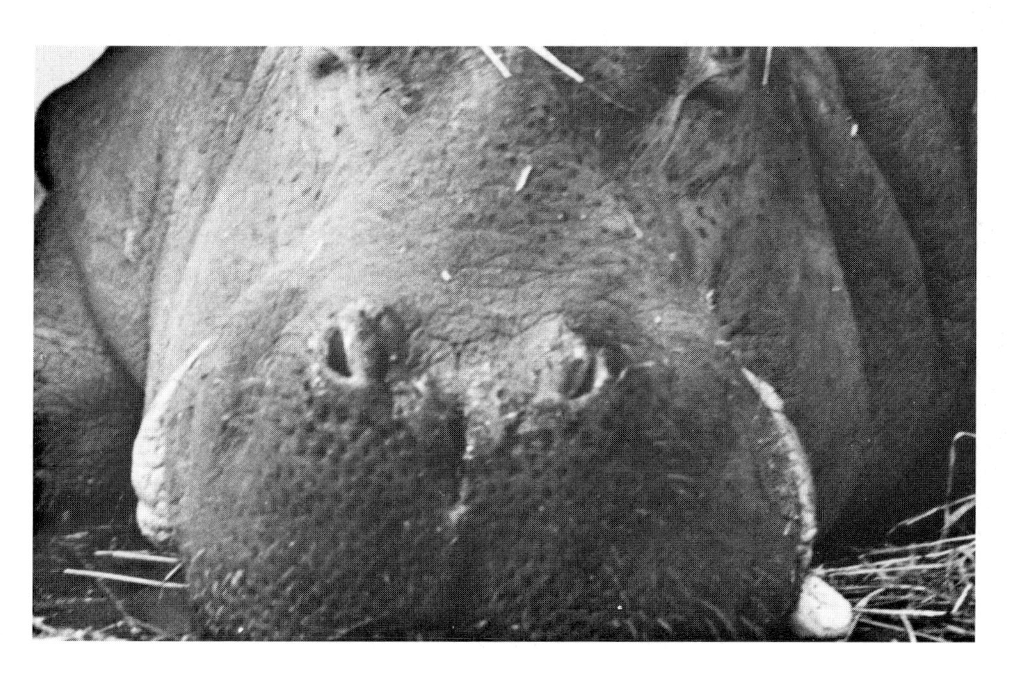

My hide is quite tough and I'm ugly and gray;
I casually yawn at my troubles.
I wallow and wade in the muddiest pools,
And when I submerge, I blow bubbles.
Who am I?

Hippopotamus

Water, dear Water, I love you, Water!
You're wet and you're filled with fish.
My flippers I'll flap and my tail I will slap,
You're everything that I could wish.
Who am I?

Seal

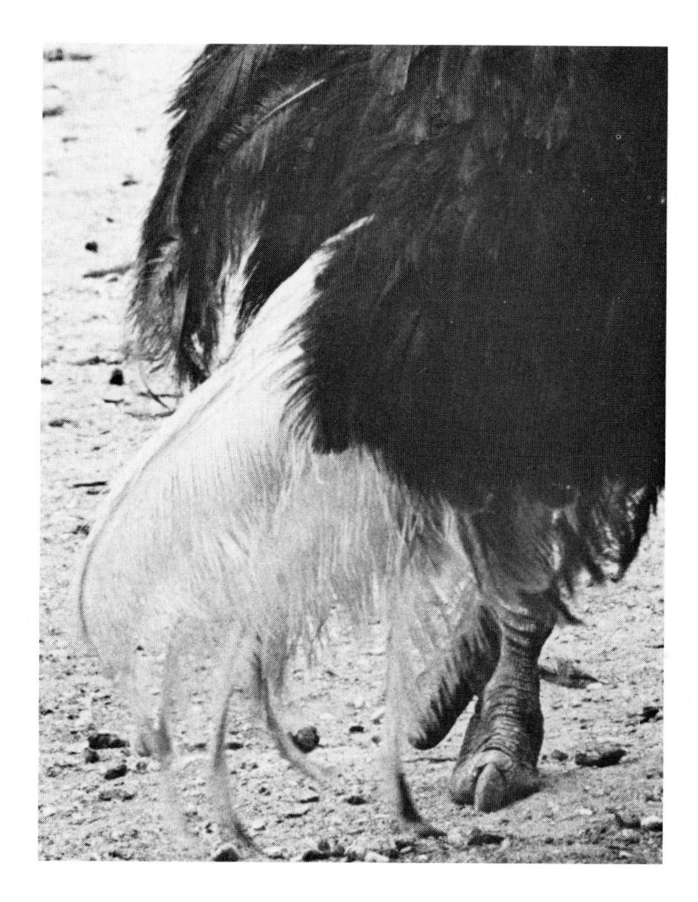

Whenever I bury my head in the sand
I'm filled with birdish glee.
Because when I find I can't see you
I'm sure you can't see me!
Who am I?

Ostrich

My markings are handsome, I tell myself,
Though I find them most perplexing.
I *think* that I'm white with stripes of black,
But I can't be sure, and it's vexing.
Who am I?

Zebra

My temper's a terror, I hate the world.
I'll charge any object in view!
But if you had a horn on the end of your nose
And your vision was poor—wouldn't you?
Who am I?

Rhinoceros

Spotted silence in the night—
I stalk my prey through pale moonlight.
I have a green unwinking stare;
My paws hide daggers, so beware!
Who am I?

Leopard

I'll dance for a supper of wild honeycomb.
In the winter I sleep without pauses.
Though I'm famous for hugs, I'm also the creature
That when you wake up, you're as cross as.
Who am I?

Bear

I've soft brown spots on yellow skin,
My neck is very long and thin.
I am so marvelously tall
I hardly see the ground at all.
Who am I?

Giraffe

The men among us wear the crowns.
You'll seldom see us close to towns.
But should you hike a mountainy "proppity"
You'll find what Indians call the wapiti.
Who am I?

Wapiti

I'm Danger lurking close to waters warm,
Be wise, and view me with profound alarm.
Beware my teeth! But should *they* miss their mark,
My flailing tail will put you in the dark.
Who am I?

Crocodile

A finicky, funny, furry guest
From far-off China I come to you.
To gain my friendship I suggest
You tickle my tastebuds with bamboo.
Who am I?

Panda

I carry the freight on Andean slopes
Where cars or trucks can't get it to.
My coat's a very good source of wool
But my temper is bad and I'll spit at you.
Who am I?

Llama

I skulk and sneak and steal and snicker
Across the plains of wild Africa.
My greed I feed when I go a-rovering,
The lunch I munch is a lion's leftovering.
Who am I?

Hyena

I am a bird who cannot fly,
But I can swim just like an eel.
I dress in formal black and white
To dine upon my seafood meal.
Who am I?

Penguin

Bill was his name and his game was my name
When I roamed in my home in the West.
I was hunted off my plains, my herds fled before
the trains,
So my picture on a nickel is the way you know me
best.
Who am I?

Bison

My feet can run or skip or hop.
They very seldom walk.
My mind is full of "Whys?" and "Hows?"
That spill out when I talk.
Who am I?

You

A curtain call is on the stage.
To see it you must turn the page.

Lion The lion's lordly appearance and big, loud roar have earned him the name "King of Beasts." While other members of the cat family live alone or in pairs, the lion moves about in a group called a "pride." Lions are found in Africa and in a very small part of India. They live on the dry open plains where they sleep by day and hunt by night. Usually it is the female, or lioness, who does the killing. Lions kill only when hungry and share the food with each other. They fill up on antelope or zebra until they are stuffed and then may wait several days before hunting again.

Kangaroo These wonderful animals come from Australia. There, the grown males are called "boomers," the females "flyers," and the babies "joeys." When a "joey" is born, he is tiny and helpless. His mother puts him in her pouch right away where he can eat, sleep and grow up in safety. Later the "joey" will leave the pouch to run and play and eat, but if he's frightened or tired he will jump back in. Kangaroos can leap fast and far on their powerful hind legs. Their long, strong tails are used to help balance them as they bound along. Kangaroos are shy by nature but if attacked they are fierce fighters. They grasp their enemy with their forefeet and then kick him with their mighty hind feet.

Camel Camels are called the ships of the desert because they can walk with ease over the great sandy wastes of North Africa and Asia. There are many things about a camel that make this possible. For instance, the wall of one of the camel's three stomachs stores up to one and a half gallons of water. Also, his feet have cushioned pads for walking in the sand. The camel's humps are made of fats that act as food when he can find nothing to eat. So when a camel goes on a trip he takes extra water and food with him and his feet don't tire easily. But camels' tempers are not good. When cross, they may bite or spit at you.

Monkey Monkeys are members of a group called the primates. Some other members are Man and Apes. The monkey in the picture is a vervet. He comes from Africa. Monkeys spend most of their time in trees. They have great curiosity and are friendly and smart. They are natural athletes and some monkeys even enjoy swimming and diving. The greatest monkey athlete is the spider monkey of South America, who truly does use his tail as a fifth hand. Most monkeys are vegetarians, but some eat insects and eggs. They are sociable creatures who live in family groups. They have very keen sight and some even see colors which is rare in animals.

Elephant The African elephant is the world's largest land animal, measuring up to 11½ feet at the shoulder and weighing six to eight tons. Elephants travel in herds of a few to a hundred. They shuffle along in single file from one waterhole to the next, leaving behind a smooth path marked by broken branches and barkless trees. They eat at least 350 pounds of leaves and grass and drink 50 gallons of water a day. Did you know that elephants are either right- or left-handed, that they can slide down a hill on their bellies, or that they can sleep standing up?

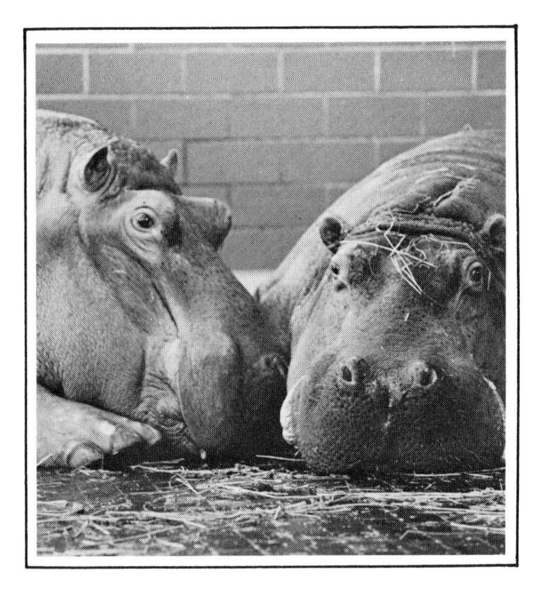

Hippopotamus Though "hippopotamus" means "river horse," this strange animal is a member of the pig family. It is certainly the biggest member, sometimes weighing four tons. It is second in weight to the elephant and its mouth is second in size to the whale's. It can spout like a whale when it comes to the surface of the African lake or river where it lives at peace with the crocodile. Crocodiles are afraid of hippos. Hippos can stay under water for 30 minutes. They eat water plants, reeds and grass but also raid nearby vegetable gardens at night. A hippo named Pete, who lived in the Bronx Zoo, ate 90 pounds of hay and 36 pounds of soup a day. Very piggy.

Seal Seals have three things in common with dogs. They bark, their babies are called pups and they make good pets. They are graceful and tireless in the water but don't move easily on land. Seals eat fish they catch while swimming. They are at home in the water, and yet a seal pup must be taught to swim by its mother. Seals come ashore to sleep and sunbathe. They are found in all seas of the world except the Indian Ocean, and sometimes they follow schools of fish up rivers. They are curious and friendly and are said to love music.

Ostrich The ostrich is sometimes called the "camel bird" because of its long neck and clumsy walk. Like the camel, it can go for a long time without water. This is important because it lives mostly in the dry plains and sandy deserts of Africa. The ostrich is the largest living bird. A big male stands eight feet tall and weighs 300 pounds. Ostriches can't fly, but they can run at least 40 miles an hour. Kicking as well as running is a defense for this bird. Contrary to popular belief, they do not bury their heads in the sand, but when nesting they stretch their necks flat along the ground if danger is near.

Zebra The zebra comes from Africa. There are several kinds of zebras, but they all have those beautiful black stripes. The zebra in our riddle is a Grevy's zebra which is the biggest kind. It is the size of a small horse. Others are Burchell's zebra, the true or mountain zebra and Grant's zebra. They travel in herds, some in the mountains, some on the plains. Whenever you see a herd of zebras you know you can find water nearby, because they never stray far from a drinking hole. Zebras are very watchful and can run very fast, which is a good thing because they are a lion's favorite dinner.

Rhinoceros Rhinos are big clumsy animals with thick saggy skin that looks like armour-plating and legs that are too short. They are very nearsighted, yet have a keen sense of hearing and smell. The bad-tempered black rhinoceros in our riddle will charge almost anything—even a railroad train. He has two large horns made of matted hair that grow throughout his life. The black rhinoceros is a loner who lives on the dry plains and rocky hillsides of Africa feeding mainly on bushes and twigs. He is a good swimmer and loves to wallow in the mud and bathe in dust. The black rhino is one of five species living in Africa or Asia.

Leopard Leopards come from Africa and Asia. They are as dangerous as they are beautiful. They can swim, climb or jump with great ease. They hunt almost all the time and are silent, deadly trackers. After a kill leopards will often carry their victim up into a tree where they may eat in safety. Their spotted coat was designed by nature to help these clever cats remain unseen by their prey. It is such a perfect camouflage that in World War II it was copied by the U.S. Army and used for jungle warfare. The black leopard also has spots, though they are hard to see.

Bear The polar bear is mainly a meat eater, though at times he will eat seaweed, grass or other plants. Living in Arctic lands, he has thick fur and an extra layer of fat to protect him from the cold. His feet are furry on the bottom to keep him from slipping on the ice. He is the swimmer of the bear family and catches fish and baby seals. He hunts on land, too. The European brown bear in the riddle picture is particularly fond of honey and rarely eats meat. He lives in Europe's forests and can climb trees. He sleeps from about November to March each year.

Giraffe

Long, long ago, travelers returning to Rome from Africa told of a beast they called "camelopard." They said it had spots like a leopard and a neck like a camel. Today we know they had seen a giraffe. The giraffe is the tallest of all living creatures. It has been known to grow as tall as 20 feet. Since its favorite food is leaves of the acacia tree, being tall is a big help at meal time. In an acacia grove, the giraffe's spots look like blotches of light and shadow, hiding the animal from sight. The giraffe can go a month without water because it gets moisture from the leaves it eats. It is sometimes hunted by the lion, but mostly lions prefer to attack weaker animals.

Wapiti

Named by the Indians, this beautiful American deer is second in size only to the moose. A full-grown male weighs as much as 700 pounds and stands five feet tall at the shoulder. The wapiti lives in North America and is mostly seen in the western United States and Canada, though once it was common from coast to coast. Wapitis eat grass, leaves and buds. The male has antlers which he sheds once a year. Friendly and easily trained to live with people, wapitis have sometimes learned to pull carts, and "trotting elks" have been shown at country fairs in the past.

Crocodile The crocodile is one of the largest living reptiles. It is found in tropical countries throughout the world. Crocodiles like big shallow lakes, ponds and rivers, and often float with only their eyes and nose showing above the water. They can swim with surprising speed and also can walk well on land. Crocodiles are sometimes mixed up with alligators, but one can easily tell them apart. The crocodile has a big lower tooth on each side which can be seen even when his mouth is shut. This makes him look almost as if he is grinning. Crocodiles eat fish and many kinds of animals.

Panda Giant pandas come from the mountain jungles of Szechuan province in westernmost China, and from corners of neighboring Tibet and Nepal. They are not often seen, even in the bamboo forests where they live by themselves. They are thought to be "crepuscular"—meaning that they are awake and busy at sunrise and sunset. Full-grown giant pandas weigh about 300 pounds and are as much as six feet long, but a panda cub when it is born weighs only *five ounces!* These young pandas grow fast. By their first birthday, they have gained 80 pounds and are ready to take care of themselves. Grown pandas eat 20 pounds of food a day, mostly bamboo. They sit to eat, holding bamboo shoots with their five-fingered paws and extra-long wrist bones which act much like thumbs. Their throats and stomachs have a special lining which protects them from bamboo splinters. Their fur is thick and rough with an oily undercoat that keeps them warm and dry in rain, snow and cold. They also have hair on the bottom of their paws to help them walk on the snow and ice. In zoos, pandas are playful and fun-loving, but they seem to get a bit cranky as they grow old.

Llama A native of the Andean mountain range of South America, the llama has been a friend and servant to man for at least 4,000 years. He is the only pack animal native to the New World. The full-grown llama weighs about 300 pounds and can carry from 75 to 100 pounds of goods about 20 miles a day over rough mountain country. A member of the camel family, the llama's stomach has three compartments, one of which stores food as the animal eats. Then, when he is resting, that food is brought up and he chews it again. If he is angry, the llama will spit this cud in his enemy's face. A llama's coat can be used for wool but is not as valued as the coats of his cousins, the alpaca and vicuna. Llamas like high places and are happiest when living at 8,000 feet or more above sea level.

Hyena The hyena lives in Africa, the Middle East, Asia Minor, and western India. There are three kinds: the spotted hyena, the striped hyena, and the brown hyena. This animal looks like a dog, but is more closely related to the cat. Its hind legs are shorter and weaker than its forelegs, and so it is a slow runner and can catch only sick, hurt, old or very young animals. The hyena is also a scavenger, which means it eats what other animals have left. It is very important in keeping a balance in nature because it gets rid of the sick and weak. Hyenas have the strongest jaws of all the world's animals. They live in packs which range in size from 10 to 60 hyenas. They usually hunt at night and sleep during the day. A hyena's sounds include doglike yips, whines and barks, but once in a while it "laughs" in a series of wild cackles, howls, and hoots.

Penguin Long, long ago, in many parts of the Southern Hemisphere, some birds called penguins learned to live in the water. They became so at home in the sea that they had no need to fly and little by little they lost that ability. Today's penguins still have wings, but the wings are small and are used as flippers. When on land, penguins stand upright and walk, run or hop. Sometimes they slide on their stomachs, pushing themselves along with their flippers. Penguins sleep and eat in the water. They come ashore only when it is the time of year to lose their old feathers and grow new ones or to raise a family. Penguins are very good parents. The father takes care of the single egg once it is laid. He keeps it warm for two months while the mother goes back to the ocean to feed. When the baby chick arrives, the mother comes back to help the father. They take two-week turns caring for it until the chick is old enough to feed itself. Then the whole family goes to sea together.

Bison The bison is the most famous of all American animals. It is often called a buffalo which is wrong; a true buffalo has no hump. A big male bison weighs as much as a ton and stands six feet high at the shoulder. Bison are grass-eating animals. Before colonists came to this land, the bison's range was all of North America. Floods, fires, earthquakes and storms were their only enemies. Before 1800, 50 million of the big shaggy animals roamed the land. But as people moved across America, the bison's numbers grew smaller. By 1900, there were only 300 left alive. Then laws were passed to protect them. Now there are more than 30,000.

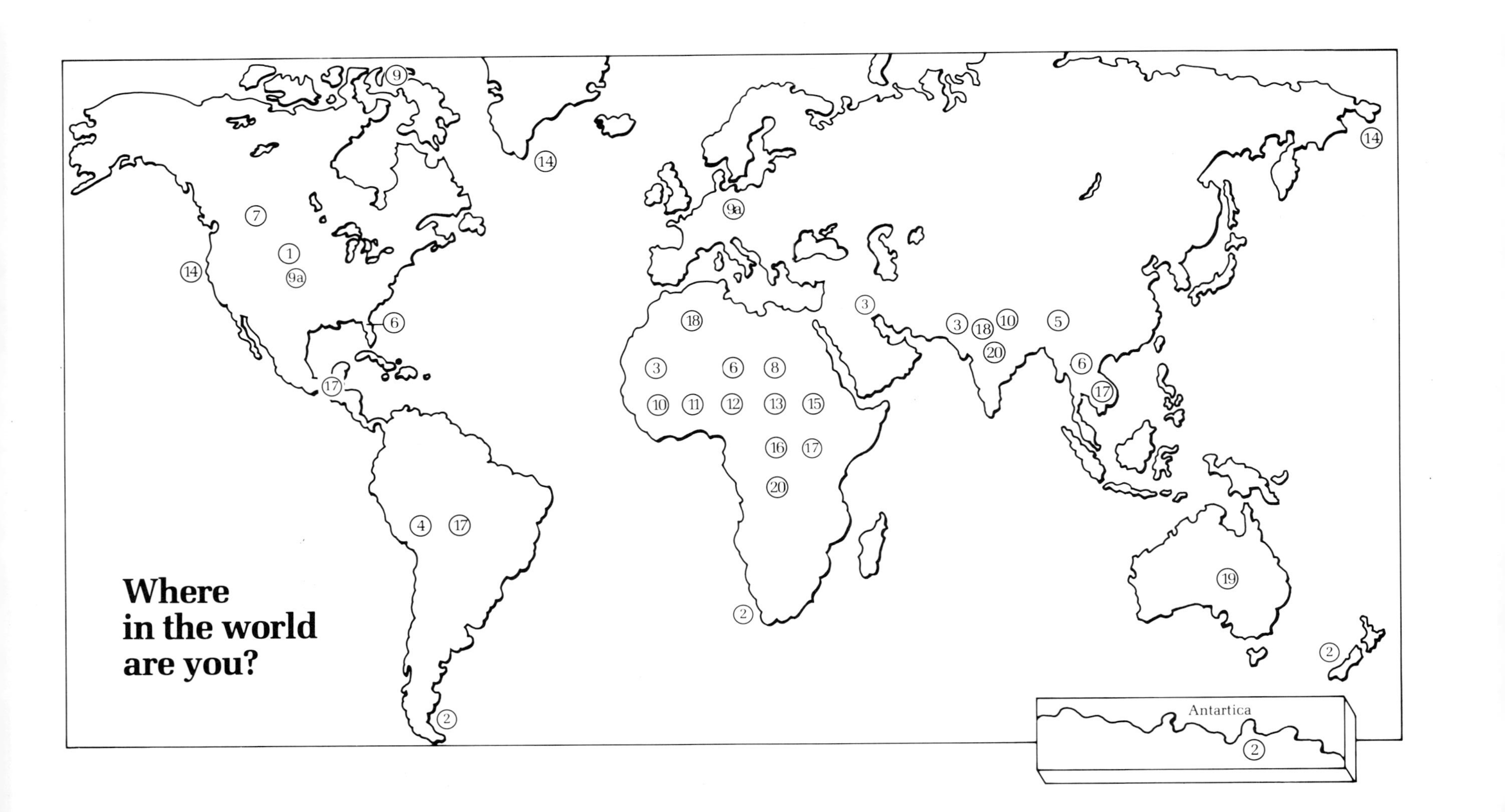
Where
in the world
are you?
Antartica

(1) Bison — North America
(2) Penguin — Antarctica, Southern Hemisphere
(3) Hyena — Africa, Middle East, India
(4) Llama — South America
(5) Panda — China, Tibet, Nepal
(6) Crocodile — North America, Africa, Asia
(7) Wapiti — North America, Canada
(8) Giraffe — Africa
(9) Polar Bear — Arctic
(9a) Brown Bear — North America, Eurasia
(10) Leopard — Africa, Asia
(11) Rhinoceros — Africa
(12) Zebra — Africa
(13) Ostrich — Africa
(14) Seal — All over the world
(15) Hippopotamus — Africa
(16) African Elephant — Africa
(17) Monkey — Africa, South and Central America, Asia
(18) Camel — North Africa, Asia
(19) Kangaroo — Australia
(20) Lion — Africa, India